To the best

Auntie

in the world

OUR JOURNAL
of your life

Dear Auntie

I'm giving you this journal so that we can share your precious memories, happy events, funny stories, awkward moments and your hopes and dreams for the future.

Whenever something pops into your head, just jot it down in the handy sections laid out. We'll have so much fun reviewing them together, and it's bound to prompt more memories.

It doesn't have to be all words. Make your journal personal with doodles, mementos and photos. You'll find a pocket at the back where you can safely store tickets, invitations, postcards and other scrapbook souvenirs so they'll never be lost.

I can't wait to share your journal with you.

All About You

BAE - Best Auntie Ever

What inspires you?

What gets you up in the morning?

Tell me all about you. What is your first memory? What was it like at home growing up. Who was your best friend when you were young? How did you wear your hair? Don't leave anything out!

x X x

When I was born, my world was like this…

My first wheels

newsflash!

beautiful baby

Me as a baby

Date of birth:

Place of birth:

I was named:

My pet name is:

First word:

hair shade

Brown eyes
or blue?

This is how I'd describe myself...

Me,
aged:

marvellous me!

My vital statistics

Height:

Weight:

Dress size:

Shoe size:

I grew up in a place called…

I've lived in:

My first house

My first home
address

Street:

Town:

County:

My school days were...

schoolgirl crush

life-changing book

My best subjects:

school clubs

My worst subjects:

Great teacher:

Terrible teacher:

Best days!

My teenage style icon was…

clothes

trendy shops

shoes

makeup

accessories

In my spare time, I like to…

pastime

hobbies

exercise

My passion...

Well Auntie, I've finished reading your first chapter, but I would still like to know...

Are we alike?

You and Me

A special connection!

What do we do for fun?

How old were you when I was born? What was it like when you first held me? Do your think we look alike? What's the best thing about being my Auntie? I hope you're proud of me!

x X x

It was written in the stars...

_____
_____
_____
_____
_____
_____
_____
_____
_____
_____
_____
_____
_____
_____
_____
_____
_____
_____
_____

star sign

You and me

Compatibility

My birthday:

My birth sign:

Your birthday:

Your birth sign:

I remember when…

I first
baby-sat
you

your first
birthday

our first
shopping trip

We are alike...

_____

_____

_____

_____

_____

_____

_____

_____

_____

_____

you, aged:

cute smile

Me at your age

We are different...

_____

_____

_____

_____

_____

_____

_____

_____

_____

_____

face shape

Some of the things we like doing together...

Remember when we...

cooking

 movies

 makeup

Auntie: What time?
Me: 9:30 😐
Auntie: Good luck!
Let me know how
it goes x

 texting

You and I were together when...

_____

_____

_____

_____

_____

_____

_____

_____

_____

_____

_____

sleepover

Some things my mum
taught me that I'll always
remember:

mishap

special
occasions

holiday

I'm proud of you because you're...

funny

helpful

What makes
you so special:

You

beautiful

clever

kind

We might disagree about...

_____
_____
_____
_____
_____
_____
_____
_____

Auntie, there are a couple of things you missed out that I thought of...

Family and Friends

The cast list! ↗

Any family secrets?

Whose shoulder do you cry on?

What do you remember about your parents when you were growing up? How did you get on with my parents? Did you have a cool auntie? You can tell me anything!

My family tree...

grandpa

grandma

Taken when...

mum dad

pets

↖ Taken when...

Siblings can be good company.
They can also be very annoying...

sisters
brothers

<u>List of annoying things...</u>

Together

Some of our relations are lovely…

aunties

Notable relations:

Some of our relations are seriously weird…

uncles

Skeleton in the
cupboard…

cousins

we never
mention…

On a scale of one to ten, your mum and dad are…

cool

↖ How we laughed!

crazy

sane

↖ Me and my siblings

_____

_____

_____

_____

_____

_____

_____

_____

_____

_____

cringeworthy

My best friend at school was... *the things we did!*

Me and my shadow

Best night ever!

Where:

When:

Who was there:

best singalong

our most-played
boxset

My first boyfriend was…

first kiss

photo taken in:

He was aged:

I was aged:

We were friends for:

fun memories

So, Auntie, our family tree would look like this...

Magical Moments

what are the high points?

You had to be there!

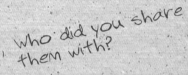

who did you share them with?

When did you fall in love? What's the wildest place you've ever visited? Have you ever felt really proud of yourself? Share your special moments.

The final year of school was so...

_____

_____

_____

_____

_____

_____

_____

_____

_____

_____

Brilliant!

Party Invitation

When:

Where:

Who came:

The happiest Christmas we shared…

_____

_____

_____

_____

_____

_____

_____

_____

_____

_____

_____

_____

_____

_____

_____

_____

_____

_____

_____

white Christmas

Christmas
tree

A very
Merry
Christmas →

My best holiday ever...

_____

_____

_____

_____

_____

_____

_____

_____

Paradise!

sun, beach, surf

romantic
weekends
away

The best parties and festivals of my life...

Partygoers:

dance moves

tasty tipple

I must remember never to...

My soul mate…

← Love at first sight!

what he said

how we met

My wedding day…

Guest List

You are invited to
The Wedding of

....

&

....

on

....

at

....

The
happy
couple!
↙

ding! dong!

What are the special moments you're still looking forward to?

Awards and Prizes

And the winner is...

The talented one!

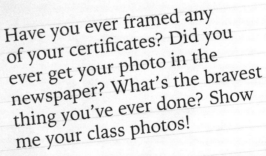

Have you ever framed any of your certificates? Did you ever get your photo in the newspaper? What's the bravest thing you've ever done? Show me your class photos!

x X x

The greatest triumphs of my life are...

_____

_____

_____

_____

_____

_____

_____

_____

_____

_____

_____

_____

_____

_____

_____

_____

 leaving home

Life events

First job ☐

First apartment ☐

First bill ☐

First house ☐

Engagement ☐

Marriage ☐

First baby ☐

touring
alone

I'm really good at…

drama

← Best in class!

 baking

quiz games

finding good gifts

I've won prizes for...

fancy dress

bingo

exams

dancing

well done me!
↓

Karaoke

CERTIFICATE

This has been awarded to

_____

The bravest thing I've ever done... *supporting a friend*

confession

rescue mission

I did it!

I'm still a bit
freaked out by...

I've set myself a target to…

Reminder…

exercise

savings

TO DO List...

I never thought I'd be able to...

_____

_____

_____

_____

_____

_____

_____

_____

_____

That's me! ↗

learn to drive

volunteer

perform in public

Oh Auntie, I think you've been a bit modest. There are lots of other accomplishments you haven't mentioned...

Dramas and Dilemmas

I will survive!

A & E

ASAP

OMG!

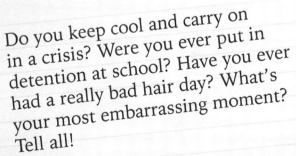

Do you keep cool and carry on in a crisis? Were you ever put in detention at school? Have you ever had a really bad hair day? What's your most embarrassing moment? Tell all!

My worst holiday nightmare was...

lost luggage

sunburn

Missed flight

Postcard from hell!

Dear

Love from

 camping
catastrophe

I can't believe I said that...!

it wasn't me!

Top 10 embarrassing moments:

awkward!

oops!

I'll never live it down!

Did I ever tell you about the time…?

Saved!

spilt milk

accidents &
emergencies

not again!

I can't believe I got away with it…

fashion fiasco

style slip up

message deleted!

sent mail

Mouth malfunction:

Who:

When:

What:

_____
_____
_____
_____
_____
_____
_____
_____
_____
_____
_____
_____

I'm only telling you about this so you don't make the same mistakes...

_____

_____

_____

_____

_____

_____

_____

_____

_____

_____

_____

_____

_____

_____

missed appointments

getting lost

spending spree

I wish I hadn't...

I trusted them!

Some things make me sad…

Always on
my mind

Auntie, it's good to know that, whatever happens, you'll always overcome it. How do you think it might have changed you?

strawberry or lemon?

Top Stuff

Apart from me obviously!

Brad Pitt or Johnny Depp?

What's your special song? Which actress do you admire most? What's the best book you've ever read? Which would you choose: strawberry or chocolate, diamond or ruby, high heels or flats? I'd like to know all your likes and dislikes.

x X x

My top ten songs of all time are…

top artist

Best live concert!

most listened to

My best-ever movie is...   costume drama

_____

_____

_____

_____

_____

_____

_____

_____

_____

_____

adventure

Top ten films...

fantasy

My number one author is…

_____

_____

_____

Must-read books…

Helen Fielding

J. K. Rowling

Alice Munro

Maya Angelou

Daphne du Maurier

My food to drool over is...

_____

_____

_____

_____

_____

_____

_____

_____

Black fore
gateau

Best
restaurant!

Japanese cuisine

strawberries and champagne

breakfast in bed

My special place is…

_____

_____

_____

_____

_____

_____

_____

_____

_____

_____

_____

_____

home sweet home

Luxury!

I couldn't live without…

treats

pet

tea  coffee

laptop

Auntie, now I know some of the things you love best, do you have a secret wish list of things you've always wanted but never had?

Ideas to Live By

Tried and tested ↗

The best is
yet to come!

Seize the day!

What is your viewpoint on life?
Do you have a significant proverb?
Are there any sayings that help you
through difficult moments? Who
do you turn to for advice? Pass on
your wisdom to me!

x X x

My philosophy of life is…

_____

_____

_____

_____

_____

_____

_____

_____

_____

_____

_____

_____

_____

_____

_____

_____

_____

Keep smiling!

Think on...

A journey starts
with a single step.

Worrying never
solved anything.

The difference
between 'ordinary'
and 'extraordinary'
is just that little
'extra'.

Yes, I CAN!

The world would be a better place if...

...shopping solved anything

...I spent less time on social media

...I could learn to love waterproofs

no litter

recycle

My pet rants...

stop global warming
end poverty

Some of the proverbs and sayings that help me...

Actions speak louder than words.

Two wrongs don't make a right.

Laughter makes
the world go
round.

Be the change
you wish for.

My brilliant expressions…

The things people say:

No way!

Life's too short!

No problem!
Give me a break!

If life has taught me anything, it's…

Be the solution, not the problem.

Focus on what matters.

Think positive!

All I need is
friendship and
sunshine.

These are the values I try to live by…

Life lessons:

Be truthful

face new challenges

Put others first

Make amends

kindness
courage
honesty
loyalty
patience

Dear Auntie, I never knew you were so wise! What's the single most useful advice for life you can pass on to me?

Bucket List

Your life's ambitions

action plan

hopes and dreams

Tell me about the things you're hoping to do. Are there any new activities you're going to try out? Plan a family reunion? Write a novel? Adopt a penguin? Visit Timbuktu? Don't put it off!

x X x

These are the places I'd most love to visit...

Itch list:

I'd like to try my hand at...

learn to juggle

kayaking

wall climbing

weaving

I did it!

I'm determined to...

stay
fit

do a road trip

learn wine tasting

go on a walking weekend

master
bread making

My personal goals are...

_____
_____
_____
_____
_____
_____
_____
_____
_____
_____
_____
_____
_____
_____

be mindful

declutter

My goal schedule:

Together we can…

_____

_____

_____

_____

_____

_____

_____

_____

_____

_____

Activities for two:

pondej!

PULTENEY PRESS

First published by Pulteney Press in 2019
Copyright © Pulteney Press 2019
Written by Katherine Sully • Illustrated by Michael Cheung,
All other images 123rf

ISBN 978-1-78838-885-6

Printed in China

Dear

Love Auntie x